The Window of Life

Discussion Questions

Lin Zittel

Based on the book by Annelisa Stephen

Cover page by Gracelyn Stephen

ISBN: 979-8-3387-8646-8

Part One Questions

<u>Chapter 1:</u>

    1. Based on the book's title, what do you think the author, Annelisa, hopes to show you in these pages? (Hint: Define window, life, and journey) What is the Book of Acts?

_____

_____

_____

_____

_____

_____

    2. Under most chapter headings throughout the book, Annelisa gives a Bible reference to give the reader a real-life background for her story-telling. Do you plan to read these parallel passages? Why or why not?

_____

    3. What do you know about Eutychus from Chapter One?

_____

_____

_____

_____

_____

_____

****

<u>Chapter 2:</u>

    1. On page 11, Eutychus has compassion for the lame man. Has God given you compassion for those less fortunate than you? What is one thing you would do to show someone needy the love Jesus has for him or her?

_____

_____

_____

_____

_____

2. Look carefully at how Peter addressed the crowd on page 13. Eutychus admired Peter's boldness. Why did his speech show boldness? How can you be bold when sharing about Jesus?

_____

_____

_____

_____

_____

_____

3. How is Eutychus' relationship with his earthly dad like that of the Heavenly Father?

_____

_____

_____

_____

_____

_____

****

Chapter 3:

1. Eutychus is worried about leaving the only home he has ever known to move to Jerusalem. If your family suddenly had to move, what kinds of questions would you have?

_____

_____

_____

_____

_____

2. How did Eutychus console himself (on page 24) regarding the move?

_____

_____

_____

_____

_____

_____

3. Silvanus suggested the boys eavesdrop on their parents. Why was Eutychus uncomfortable with this? Have you ever given in to the pressure of friends against your better judgment? What happened?

4. What was the most important reason Eutychus' father gave for doing anything? (p. 28)

****

Chapter 4:

1. Before Eutychus left his home, he surveyed his house. If you were moving away tomorrow, what places in your home would you want to "hold" with your eyes one last time?

2. Eutychus "mulled over" Proverbs 19:21, which his father quoted. That means he thought hard about the meaning of the verse. What is the benefit of meditating or thinking hard about Scripture?

3. Eutychus' name meant fortunate. Do you know the meaning of your name? Does its meaning fit your personality?

_____
_____

4. What promise did the angels give the disciples as Jesus ascended into heaven? (p. 34)

_____
_____
_____
_____

****

Chapter 5:

1. Eutychus wondered how Matthew, the tax collector, changed. Describe Matthew's transformation and how you believe he was changed.

_____
_____
_____
_____
_____
_____

2. What sin did Ananias and his wife commit? Why did God judge them by taking their lives? (p. 41, Peter's explanation).

_____
_____
_____
_____
_____

3. What law did Caiaphas accuse the disciples of breaking? What would you do if you were jailed for telling someone the Gospel?

_____
_____
_____
_____
_____
_____

****

Chapter 6:

1. Memorize Acts 5:29b. "We ought to obey God rather than men." Does this mean we are free to break the laws established by our government? What does it mean?

   _____
   _____
   _____
   _____
   _____
   _____

2. Eutychus knew that Jesus had seen and known about him before he was born. (p. 47). The same is true about you. Read Psalm 139:1-4,13-18. How does that make you feel?

   _____
   _____
   _____
   _____

3. On page 49, Eutychus witnessed Caiaphas' reaction to the officers' report that the disciples were no longer imprisoned. Why did he want to remember the look on Caiaphas' face forever?

   _____
   _____
   _____

4. What was Gamaliel's proposed solution to the "problem" of the disciples' bold teaching of the Gospel (Good News)?

   _____
   _____
   _____

****

Chapter 7:

1. The Bible warns believers not to be "yoked" with unbelievers. Why do you think it was important for the men chosen as overseers of the food distribution to be "of good reputation, full of the Holy Spirit and wisdom"? (p. 56)

_____
_____
_____
_____
_____

2. Read the first paragraph at the top of page 57. Eutychus felt
    God's presence while the group prayed. Describe a time when
    you were in God's presence. If you are unsure of how Eutychus
    felt, pray and ask the Lord's Spirit to make Himself known to
    you.

_____
_____
_____
_____
_____
_____

3. Why do you think Stephen gave God the credit for changing
    Joshua? (p. 62). Have you ever felt like "an instrument in
    God's hand"?

_____
_____
_____
_____
_____
_____

****

Chapter 8:
1. The chapter is titled "Exiled." Let's look up the meaning of
    "exiled." Could you have guessed what might have happened in
    this chapter just by reading the title?

_____
_____

2. Look again at Stephen's great explanation of the Pharisees'
    objection to Jesus on page 66. Let's pray to reflect Stephen's
    attitude and words to one of your friends who is an unbeliever.
    Tell your friends about this book, and invite them to learn

more about Jesus. Tell why you know Jesus loves you and loves your friend.

_____
_____
_____
_____
_____
_____

3. On pp. 68-70, Caiaphas pointed out some beliefs he thought were true. He even referenced Scriptures that describe the Jewish Messiah. How did Joshua refute Caiaphas' mistaken beliefs?

_____
_____
_____
_____
_____
_____

4. What price did Joshua pay for boldly standing for Christ?

_____
_____
_____
_____

****

Chapter 9:

1. Stephen was accused of blasphemy. Look up and define "blasphemy". Was this a true or false accusation of Stephen? How do you know?

_____
_____
_____
_____

2. Why did Stephen answer Caiaphas by telling the Israelites' history? (See Tychicus' answer at the bottom of p. 76.)

_____

_____

_____

3. By what power could Stephen forgive the angry mob that stoned him?

_____

4. The Lord did not save Stephen from a horrific death. But what blessing did Stephen receive as he was being delivered through the hatred, lies, and destruction of the enemy, Satan?

_____

_____

_____

_____

****

Chapter 10:

1. As you read Eutychus' mother's description of Job's experience on pp. 80-81, point out the contrast between what Job suffered and the blessings amid his suffering.

_____

_____

_____

_____

_____

_____

2. How did Stephen's martyrdom affect Eutychus personally? How did Peter encourage him? Define martyr.

_____

_____

_____

_____

_____

_____

3. Eutychus believed, "Bad people should be punished," and he could not understand how Stephen could ask God to forgive

his murderers. How did Peter explain the amazing power God gives us to forgive?

_____

_____

_____

_____

_____

_____

4. What does Peter assure Eutychus about the purpose of testing? (p. 85) Have you experienced a test that has strengthened your faith in God?

_____

_____

_____

_____

_____

_____

****

Chapter 11:

1. The disciples took comfort in remembering that Jesus had prepared them to expect persecution because the world hated Him, and so would also hate them. How do you think remembering Jesus' words brought them encouragement and comfort? (Hint: Jesus always gave a promise with absolute truths, i.e., "I have overcome the world.")

_____

_____

_____

_____

2. How could Eutychus tell that Tychicus' shop was a special place? Do you have a quiet place where you can think and pray?

_____

_____

_____

_____

3. How did Tychicus know Saul's plans against Jews of the Way would fail? (p. 92).

_____

_____

****

Chapter 12:

1. A man named Simon believed in the Lord Jesus but thought he could buy God's power from the apostles. Why did Peter have to reprimand him sharply?

_____

_____

_____

_____

2. Describe two different results that fire from heaven might have on someone. (p. 96).

_____

_____

_____

_____

_____

3. What are some blessings that come from the persecution of God's church? (pp. 96-97).

_____

_____

_____

_____

_____

4. Can you find five amazing ways God orchestrated Philip's meeting with the Ethiopian man?

_____

_____

_____

_____

_____

_____

5. Eutychus prayed and asked the Lord to help him trust God and wait patiently for His will to be done. What are you waiting for God to do?

_____

_____

_____

****

Chapter 13:

1. This chapter is pivotal, meaning it shows a great turning point. Where does Jesus Himself turn the persecution upside down?

_____

_____

_____

2. Reread what Eutychus' father says about shining God's light at the bottom of page 101. What will others see when Jesus works in our hearts? What must we do for people who hurt us?

_____

_____

_____

_____

3. On page 108, Saul says, "God chose me to be His witness." How has God made you a witness for Jesus? Saul used the words "grace, forgiveness, mercy, saved from sin and death." Using these words in a personal application to your own life, how would you explain your relationship with Jesus Christ? This is your testimony, and you must use it to draw others to Christ.

_____

_____

_____

_____

_____

_____

_____

****

Chapter 14:

1. Saul was not disturbed by having to flee and leave Jerusalem to escape the Hellenists' threat to his life. How could he remain calm under such a threat?

_____
_____
_____
_____

2. Why is it so wonderful that Gentiles were allowed to join the young church that was started with Jews only?

_____
_____
_____
_____
_____

3. Explain the miracles Peter described in Lydda and Joppa. What town do you live in? Can you imagine God turning everyone in your town away from sin to live for Christ? God is looking for someone like you to pray for the revival of his/her town. He can save a whole town!

_____
_____
_____
_____
_____

****

Chapter 15:

1. What was the significance of Peter being led to Simon's house since Jews looked down on tanners who dealt with animal skins?

_____
_____
_____
_____
_____

2. Isn't it cool how God builds one stone upon another in our lives? Peter had a dream while in a tanner's house, teaching Peter that God accepts everybody. The dream revealed a message that "What God has cleansed you must not call common." Then, he was led to a Roman soldier's house. God reinforced His message to Peter that he was to now preach to Gentiles, not just to Jews. What amazing conclusion did Eutychus reach on page 116 after hearing Peter's experience?

_____
_____
_____

3. What was the new name the people of Antioch called the young church? Do you consider yourself a Christian? Why or why not?

_____
_____
_____
_____

****

Chapter 16:

1. Why was James going to be terribly missed? (Look at the descriptions on the bottom of page 123 and the second paragraph on page 125.)

_____
_____
_____
_____
_____

2. How did James' example affect the soldier assigned to guard him?

_____
_____
_____
_____

3. How did Eutychus and the disciples experience God's grace after James' death despite the threat to their lives?

_____

_____

_____

_____

****

Chapter 17:

1. How did Silvanus' little goat, Benji, remind Eutychus' father of Adam and Eve?

_____

_____

_____

_____

_____

2. How did Eutychus answer Silvanus' suggestion that a riot might be a way to get Peter out of prison?

_____

_____

_____

_____

_____

3. Name some of the various ways in which Peter's release from prison was a miracle of God.

_____

_____

_____

_____

_____

****

Chapter 18:

1. How was King Herod heralded as he proceeded through the crowd? What does this tell you about his personality?

_____
_____
_____
_____
_____

2. What similarity did Eutychus think of between the release of
    the apostles from Caiaphas' prison and that of Peter from
    Herod's detainment?

    _____
    _____
    _____
    _____
    _____

3. How did Eutychus pray for his friend, Silvanus, as they parted
    ways? Do you think his motivation was only so Eutychus could
    prove his beliefs were right, or was there some other reason he
    prayed for him?

    _____
    _____
    _____
    _____
    _____

****

Chapter 19:
1. What evidence do you see that God took King Herod Agrippa
    out?

    _____
    _____
    _____
    _____

2. What did the letter from Saul and Barnabas reveal to Eutychus'
    parents? How did Eutychus feel about his parents' response?

_____
_____
_____
_____
_____

3. What about their future required a strong faith that God would care for and provide for them?

_____
_____
_____
_____
_____
_____

Part Two Questions

Chapter 20:
1. How did Tychicus describe his duties among the disciples? Did he seem content to perform those duties?

2. What words of wisdom did Tychicus send Eutychus off with?

3. How did John Mark's Uncle Barnabas try to ease his fears?

4. How did Saul's words put everything in perspective for Eutychus? Using a Bible map, look up where the Island of Cyprus is in relation to Antioch.

****

Chapter 21:
1. Why was John Mark so excited to show his Uncle Barnabas a letter? What is a proconsul?

2. How did Saul silence the sorcerer, Elymas? How did that action affect the proconsul?

_____
_____
_____
_____

3. How did Saul explain the reason for changing his name to Paul?

_____
_____
_____
_____
_____

****

Chapter 22:

1. What were John Mark's reasons for returning to Jerusalem? How did Paul and Barnabas attempt to dissuade him from departing?

_____
_____
_____
_____
_____
_____

2. Gentiles, called God-fearers, were allowed to worship with Jews in the synagogue. How were they different from full proselytes? (p. 161).

_____
_____
_____
_____

3. In his exhortation to those in the synagogue, Paul stated, "David died, but Jesus did not see corruption." What did he mean by that?

_____
_____
_____
_____
_____
_____

4. What bold statement did Paul make to the angry Jews (bottom of page 163)? The author, Annelisa, points out, "As the Gentiles rejoiced in their newfound freedom, the Jews were chained by their beliefs." How did the Jews exhibit signs of jealousy, pride, and hunger for control and power?

_____
_____
_____
_____
_____
_____

****

Chapter 23:

1. Why did Paul and Barnabas leave Iconium and escape to Lystra and Derbe quickly?

_____
_____

2. How did the people react to God's healing of the lame man by Paul's words? What did Paul and Barnabas do then?

_____
_____
_____
_____

3. How did the crowd change from wanting to worship the apostles to becoming eager to stone them?

_____
_____
_____
_____

****

Chapter 24:

1. Why didn't Paul decide, according to his own opinion, which mission journey to take? After all, wouldn't it be good to take the gospel anywhere?

   _____

   _____

   _____

2. At the top of page 176, Paul compliments Eutychus. What did he advise him to always have besides love and passion for God?

   _____

3. What was the argument Paul and Barnabas had to address between some Jewish Christians and the believers in Antioch? Which side of the argument makes more sense to you?

   _____

   _____

   _____

   _____

   _____

   _____

****

Chapter 25:

1. Paul reminded the elders not to look out for their own interests but also for the interests of others. Can you name one way you might look out for someone else's interests over your own?

   _____

   _____

   _____

2. Why was it so important for Peter to understand that he must not add Jewish law (rules) to Jesus' offer of salvation by grace?

   _____

   _____

   _____

   _____

3. What did John Mark learn about the work of God that caused his remorse about leaving the first mission trip (p.186)?

_____

_____

_____

_____

4. What book of the Bible did John Mark eventually write?

_____

****

Chapter 26:
1. In this chapter, Eutychus' family returns to Lystra with Paul and Barnabas. There, Eutychus met a Hebrew-speaking grandmother and her grandson, Timothy. How is Timothy described? How did they know Paul?

_____

_____

_____

_____

2. Timothy asked Paul how he felt when the people of Lystra worshipped him and, the next moment, stoned him. How did Paul answer that? (pp. 192-193).

_____

_____

_____

_____

3. How did Paul respond to God's change of direction for the missionary group? (p. 195).

_____

_____

_____

_____

_____

****

Chapter 27:

1. What is the name of the doctor who treated Eutychus for his stomach pain? Do you recognize a book of the Bible that carries his name? We also know that Dr. Luke wrote the book of Acts, which The Window of Life is based on.

   _____

2. What astounded Dr. Luke about Eutychus' recovery?

   _____

3. How did Paul know that God was directing them to Macedonia?

   _____
   _____
   _____
   _____
   _____

4. How did Paul explain water baptism? (p. 202). Have you been baptized? Why or why not?

   _____
   _____
   _____
   _____
   _____

****

Chapter 28:

1. Why did Paul disapprove of the young girl who followed them shouting, "These are the servants of the Most High God, who proclaim the way of salvation"?

   _____
   _____
   _____
   _____

2. What reasons did the girl's slave masters give for wanting to put Paul and Silas in prison?

_____
_____
_____
_____
_____

3. How long did the disciples pray while Paul and Silas were in prison? List the miracles the Lord did while they were faithfully waiting, hoping, and praying.

_____
_____
_____
_____
_____

4. How did Paul describe how God used for good the devil's intention to harm and hinder their work in God's kingdom? (p. 210).

_____
_____
_____
_____
_____

5. Why did Paul refuse to go away in secret without the authority of the magistrates to acknowledge their error?

_____
_____
_____
_____
_____

6. Which book of the Bible did Paul later write to the church at Philippi?

_____

****

Chapter 29:
1. Why did Paul leave Silas and Timothy behind in Berea? (p. 215).

_____
_____

2. How was the inscription on one of the idols an opportunity for Paul to tell about the true and living God?

_____
_____
_____
_____

3. On which major prophet did Paul base his decision to move away from Jews who would not listen?

_____

****

Chapter 30:
1. What promise did the Lord give Paul about staying in Corinth? What were the people who lived in Corinth called? Can you find two epistles in the New Testament named for them?

_____
_____
_____
_____
_____

2. Why did Gallio, the proconsul, refuse to judge the case against Paul?

_____

_____

_____

_____

3. Can anything stop God's work? Are you excited to be included in His kingdom work?

_____

****

Chapter 31:

1. Why did Paul suddenly cut his hair off after growing it long?

_____

_____

_____

_____

_____

2. What were some places Eutychus had called "home"? (p. 225).

_____

_____

_____

_____

_____

3. What happened to Silvanus? Why was his father frustrated by Silvanus' choices?

_____

_____

_____

_____

_____

4. What special item would Eutychus keep with him on future adventures and why?

_____

_____

_____

_____

****

Chapter 32:

1. How did Paul further bless the disciples he met at Ephesus who had not heard about the Holy Spirit?

2. What did Paul do when he could no longer teach in the synagogue due to those who spoke evil of the Way to the crowd assembled there?

3. What amazing way was God healing people through Paul? How did the local magicians react? (p. 237).

4. What epistle in our Bible did Paul write to the church at Ephesus?

****

Chapter 33:

1. What is ironic and very sad about Demetrius' accusation against Paul's claims that "the gods made with hands are not real"?

2. Our God requires orderly conduct, but the goddess Diana, whom the Ephesians worshiped, caused a riot. How do you sense the chaotic behavior by examining the shouts of the rioters?

_____

_____

_____

_____

3. How did the city clerk get the crowd to calm down and disperse?

_____

_____

_____

****

Chapter 34:

1. Why did Paul decide not to sail to Syria but to return through Macedonia instead?

_____

2. What clues told Eutychus that his Uncle Elijah was wealthy?

_____

_____

_____

_____

_____

3. Eutychus' father told Elijah he wasn't attracted to "the religion" of the disciples. What was he drawn to instead? (See pages 251 and 252.) How did he describe the usefulness of the law?

_____

_____

_____

_____

_____

****

Chapter 35:

1. When did you first guess that Eutychus' new acquaintance was actually Silvanus?

   _____

2. Why did Eutychus say he would not have changed any of his difficult travel experiences?

   _____
   _____
   _____
   _____
   _____

3. How did Eutychus' father know that Uncle Elijah was not yet a Christian, even though he showed some outward signs of being supportive of the church?

   _____
   _____
   _____
   _____
   _____

****

Chapter 36:

1. Paul told Eutychus that God doesn't need anyone to defend the gospel, so what motivated him to share the gospel with others?

   _____
   _____
   _____

2. If you desire the boldness to tell others about the good news of the salvation of Jesus Christ, pray Eutychus' prayer on page 262, and see what God will do!

   _____

3. Be sure to read the parallel Scripture passage, Acts 20:7-9. How did you react to this true-life account? Of what significance is "the window" in "The Window of Life"?

_____
_____
_____
_____
_____

****

Chapter 37:

1. What condition did Dr. Luke pronounce over Eutychus' body after he fell from the third-story window?

    _____
    _____

2. What realization gave Eutychus a new surge of courage and confidence to live his life as a witness for God? (p. 270).

    _____
    _____
    _____
    _____
    _____

3. What simple advice did Eutychus give his friend, Silvanus, after he declared his belief in Jesus and asked what he should do next? (p. 273).

    _____
    _____
    _____
    _____

4. What favorite saying of Paul's did Eutychus quote on page 273?

    _____

5. How has this book inspired you to read your Bible (perhaps finish the book of Acts), journal your own exciting experiences with Jesus, or pray more faithfully?

    _____
    _____
    _____
    _____

Part One Answers

Chapter 1:

1. Answers will vary. A window is described as an opening that allows light. The author, Annelisa, wants all her readers to understand that our journey in life consists of ups and downs, but when Jesus is our Lord and Savior, every situation is a window to shine His light. As Christians, we are the window of life, showing others the light of Jesus. The book of Acts is the 5th book in the New Testament, written to provide a history of the early church and detail the spread of the gospel by Jesus' disciples.

2. AWV. The author recommends that the reader pay attention to the parallel passages; nothing is better than reading God's inspired word and learning more about Him from it.

3. Eutychus is an 8-year-old boy living on a farm in Beth-Zayit (p. 3). He often daydreams and disappears from the farm every chance he gets, often causing him to fall behind in his work (p. 4). His least favorite chore is washing the bowls, but he loves to eat (p. 5). He looks for adventure and finds farm work tedious (p. 5). His favorite place to go is to a certain tree on the Mount of Olives, and his best friend is Silvanus (p. 5). He is a boy who can "hardly sit still for one minute," which causes him to have a hard time with his language studies (p. 6). He loves traveling to the market (p. 6) and desires to be as popular as the disciples of Jesus (p. 10).

Chapter 2:

1. AWV. Pray and ask God how you can show His compassion to those in need. If you can, help meet the needs of others so that you can show His love through actions and not only in words.

2. Peter's speech shows boldness because he tells the large crowd of their sin, corrects their beliefs, and gives them clear instructions on what to do next without fearing rejection, persecution, or humiliation. When we know that our message

is filled with God's hope and life for a world broken by sin, we can speak boldly because God will use our words for His glory. When we pray and ask Him for boldness to obey and glorify Him, He will empower us with His Spirit.

3. AWV. Possible responses include:

- God is all-knowing and concerned with our choices (Psalm 139). (Eutychus' father said, "I would like to ask...but I know the answer" [p. 16-17].)

- God delights in His children (Zephaniah 3:17). (Eutychus' father had a hint of laughter in his voice [p. 17].)

- God's rod and staff comfort us (Psalm 23:4), and His mercies are new (Lamentations 3:21-23). (Eutychus' father said he wouldn't punish Eutychus [p. 17].)

- God is our encourager (2 Thessalonians 2:16-17). (Eutychus' father praised his thoughtfulness [p. 17].)

- We should seek God's direction (Psalm 119:133). (Eutychus' father warned him about doing things without permission [p. 17].)

Chapter 3:

1. AWV. Possible responses might include "Where are we going?" "Why are we moving?" and "Will we be returning?"

2. Eutychus consoled himself by thinking of the adventures he would soon have. Since he had always wanted to follow the disciples around, he thought it could be fun to join them. He comforted himself with the thought that if it didn't work out, his parents could always choose to return.

3. Eutychus was uncomfortable with eavesdropping on his parents because he knew he wasn't allowed to do it and would be in trouble if his parents caught him (p. 26-27).

4. Eutychus' father's most important reason for doing anything was telling others about Jesus.

Chapter 4:
1. AWV

2. Meditating is remembering and pondering what you have heard or read. It allows you to understand better and apply God's word in your life. God tells us that we will prosper when we obey and meditate on His word (Joshua 1:8-9).

3. AWV.

4. The angels promised that the same Jesus Who was taken up into heaven would come in the same manner as they saw Him ascend. Read the account in Acts 1:4-12.

Chapter 5:
1. Matthew transformed from a tax collector usually known for cheating people to a generous man who gave money to others in need. For a bonus supplement, read the story of Zacchaeus, another tax collector, in Luke 19:1-10 and compare his transformation to Matthew's.

2. Ananias and Sapphira lied to the Lord and sought men's praise. God judged them because lying to the Holy Spirit is an offense.

3. AWV. Caiaphas accused the disciples of sinning against God by preaching about a sinner and trying to convert people from the Jewish laws (p. 43).

Chapter 6:
1. Christians are called to obey earthly authorities (Romans 13:1-2, 1 Peter 2:13–14, Titus 3:1, Hebrews 13:17) and to pray for those in power (1 Timothy 2:1–2, Romans 13:6–7). However, when our government mandates things contrary to Scripture, we are called to obey God. We must not defend sinful actions

excused by the government's laws but rather stand up for the truth of God proclaimed in His word.

2. AWV.

3. Eutychus wanted to remember Caiaphas's look because he found his shock funny and was amused by the disciples' sudden escape from jail; it was a memory that would make him laugh for years.

4. Gamaliel proposed leaving the disciples alone; if their work was of God, it couldn't be fought against, but if it were man's work, it would fade away.

Chapter 7:
1. It was important for the overseers of the food distribution to have a good reputation because they would be working with people; the people had to respect them and think well of them. It was important for the overseers to be full of the Holy Spirit and wisdom because they would need to make Spirit-led decisions and use God's wisdom in resolving conflicts and dealing with situations. If these men followed God's instructions, their ministry would succeed, and there would be fewer opinionated arguments.

2. AWV. Christians always have God's presence within them because He dwells within them (John 14:23).

3. AWV. Stephen gave God the credit because it was His work. The Holy Spirit convicts people's hearts (John 16:8) and makes us a new creation (2 Corinthians 5:17). The Father draws us (John 6:44), and He uses us to fulfill His purpose.

Chapter 8:
1. AWV. Merriam-Webster's dictionary defines "exiled" as "to banish or expel from one's own country or home."

2. AWV. Here is a sample prayer:

Lord,
Please help me show Your love to my friend who does not believe in You. Help my friend realize that You love him and died for him and that he is a sinner in need of grace. Give me the courage to tell him more about You and to help him learn more about You through Your word. Give me the words to speak Your truth, and may my actions reflect Your love so I can be Your witness.
In Jesus' Name. Amen.

3. Joshua refuted Caiaphas' mistaken beliefs by quoting Scripture in context. He understood how Jesus fulfilled the Jewish prophecies because he had studied Scripture and had a personal encounter with his Savior.

4. Joshua suffered humiliation and was stripped of his identity before being exiled. If a priest was banished, they not only were publicly shamed, but they also lost all part in Jewish society. He was forced to leave his home and his position while facing death threats from the priests.

Chapter 9:

1. Merriam-Webster's dictionary describes "blasphemy" as "the act of insulting or showing contempt or lack of reverence for God." This was a false accusation against Stephen because he revered God, and his words were filled with the Holy Spirit.

2. Tychicus explained that Stephen showed he was not against Israel's traditions and genealogy and wanted to prove that all of God's messengers had been persecuted from the beginning. By killing the Son of God, the Israelites were continuing what their ancestors had begun.

3. Stephen could only forgive the angry mob through God's power and the love of Jesus that he had experienced and

understood.

4. Stephen saw Jesus standing at the right hand of God, which reassured him of what he would be able to experience soon. He also received the power to forgive.

Chapter 10:
1. Job lost his family, his possessions, his health, and his friends were of no help. Still, he remained righteous, and amid his suffering, he received the blessing of seeing God and experiencing His faithfulness.

2. Eutychus was sorrowful, which rendered him unable to sleep. He was also confused about why God allowed Stephen to be killed and how Stephen was able to forgive his accusers. His faith was shaken because God had allowed one of his close friends to die. Peter encouraged him by urging him to share his thoughts and to trust that God's ways were higher than his and that He would always be faithful. Merriam-Webster defines a martyr as a person who voluntarily suffers death as the penalty of witnessing to and refusing to renounce a religion.

3. Peter said that Jesus enables us to give His grace and forgiveness to others. Stephen understood the love of Christ and understood that his murderers were blinded; he was so filled with Christ's love that he forgave his accusers.

4. AWV. Peter said that the purpose of testing is to strengthen our faith and make it more precious than gold. God gives us patience, perseverance, and renewed hope through our testing.

Chapter 11:
1. The disciples were comforted by Jesus' words because they proved that He knew everything that would happen in the future and still had a plan, even if the disciples didn't understand. Since Jesus always gave a promise with absolute truths, it proved that His words would never change, even if

their circumstances did.

2. AWV. Eutychus could tell that Tychicus' shop was a special place because it was cozy and well-kept. There were also hand-made items and a sketch of Tychicus' parents, which were treasured possessions.

3. Tychicus quotes a promise found multiple times in the Bible: the Lord's counsel will stand (Isaiah 46:10, Psalm 33:11, Proverbs 19:21). No matter how successful Saul's plans seemed, God's plan would be the only one to stay.

Chapter 12:

1. Peter had to sharply reprimand Simon because he was greedy for power and did not understand that the Holy Spirit came from God.

2. James and John wanted to destroy the Samaritan village with fire from heaven because they did not receive Jesus. This fire from heaven would cause destruction. When Peter and John went to the Samaritan church, the Samaritans received the Holy Spirit, which brought new life.

3. People were added to the church, and the gospel was spread to different places.

4. AWV. Some possible answers include that Philip met the eunuch at the right time, the eunuch was at the right chapter and verse for Philip to share the gospel message with him, the eunuch was ready to accept Jesus and be baptized, water appeared at the time the eunuch desired to be baptized, and Philip was taken away by the Holy Spirit so that the eunuch did not see him again.

5. AWV.

Chapter 13:

1. Jesus turns the persecution upside down when Saul, the greatest persecutor, becomes a Christian.

2. We must forgive and love the people who hurt us. When Jesus works in our hearts, others will see God's peace, joy, love, and forgiveness shining as lights through us.

3. AWV.

Chapter 14:

1. Saul was undisturbed by having to flee Jerusalem because he knew that God had great plans for him, and if he was forced to leave, God had a reason for it.

2. When the Gentiles were allowed to join the young church, it proved that God does not show partiality and that His salvation is for all!

3. AWV. In Lydda, Peter healed Aeneas, a man who had been bedridden for eight years. In Joppa, a woman named Tabitha was raised from the dead.

Chapter 15:

1. God opened Peter's heart to the truth that salvation is for all, not just for the selected Jews. We also see how God's grace triumphs over the law that forbade Jews to touch animal skins.

2. The conclusion that Eutychus came to is that God's love and mercy are for everyone.

3. AWV. The people of Antioch called the people of the church "Christians," which means followers of Christ.

Chapter 16:

1. James is described as having sparkling eyes, a loud voice, and a cheery personality. He is also described as encouraging, passionate, bold, and friendly. James was known for his loud singing and willingness to give his life for Christ. His ability to brighten the place up and encourage others would be missed.

2. The soldier was affected by James' witness, so he declared himself a Christian and was willingly executed.

3. Though there was a deep sadness, Eutychus also felt an unexplainable peace that only God could give.

Chapter 17:
1. After Adam and Eve sinned, sacrifices were required to atone for sins. The sacrifice consisted of the best of one's flock, an animal without blemish like Benji.

2. Eutychus answered that God always answers prayers. Even if it is the answer we are not expecting, God does everything for our good.

3. AWV. Some possible responses include an angel with a bright light appearing when there was full security, Peter's chains falling off, their passing the guard posts, and the iron gate opening automatically.

Chapter 18:
1. King Herod was heralded as the great and mighty king, an illustrious, splendid victor and hero, an extraordinary man with great achievements, and a remarkably impressive leader. With how King Herod reacted to the praise, we can infer that he was a proud man.

2. Caiaphas had imprisoned the disciples and the next day had sent determined officers to bring them out from jail to hold them on trial, and Herod was trying to do the same thing with

Peter. Both times, God had delivered the disciples, and both times, the disciples continued to preach.

3. Eutychus prayed that Silvanus would accept Jesus as his Lord and Savior and understand His love. Eutychus did not pray for him to prove his beliefs but prayed out of love and concern for his friend.

Chapter 19:

1. The king collapsed suddenly, and the physicians could not do anything about his condition, claiming it was a supernatural force.

2. The letter from Saul and Barnabas revealed that the Holy Spirit had instructed them to be set apart for gospel work and to depart from Antioch on a journey to spread the gospel. Although Eutychus was unsure about what lay ahead, he trusted that God's will would be done and that He would protect them, which excited him.

3. Uncertainty about their future required them to trust in the Lord. Not being in control can sometimes be very scary. As Christians, we should learn to always trust in the Lord and walk by faith, not by sight.

Part Two Answers

Chapter 20:

1. Tychicus described his duties as helping wherever and whenever possible, doing little things for God's glory. He was content to perform these duties because he knew God used every little thing.

2. Tychicus advised Eutychus to be ready for every window of opportunity the Lord gave because the Holy Spirit empowered him for God's work; he urged Eutychus never to doubt God's Spirit in him because he was called to great works.

3. Uncle Barnabas tried to ease John Mark's fears by reassuring him that their future was held in God's hands and His plan would be fulfilled.

4. Saul's words put everything in perspective for Eutychus because he stressed that God had called them and set them apart for this ministry. He was excited to get the opportunity to lay up treasures in heaven and preach about Jesus in unknown lands. It was important to remember their mission and seek what the Lord had in store for them.

Chapter 21:

1. John Mark was excited about the letter because the proconsul of Cyprus had invited them to come to Paphos so he could hear the word of God. He had heard much about Sergius Paulus and was thrilled that someone of such a high rank would want to see them. A proconsul is a governor of a province in ancient Rome who oversees the administration of civil and military matters.

2. Saul silenced Elymas by proclaiming he would be blind for a time since he would not stop perverting the ways of the Lord. When this came true, the proconsul was astonished and

believed their words.

3. God told Saul that he must become all things to all men so that he might save some. Since Saul was among the Gentiles, he felt it was necessary to be called by his Greek name.

Chapter 22:

1. John Mark was homesick, in pain, and discouraged by the few conversions that he saw. Paul and Barnabas tried to persuade him by reminding him to be faithful to the Lord's mission. They reminded him of their prayers for strength and their desire to serve God despite the hardships.

2. God-fearers were not circumcised like the Jews and did not follow all the Jewish rituals. However, they believed in God and listened in the synagogue.

3. Jesus fulfilled the Scripture in Psalm 16, where David writes, "You will not allow Your Holy One to see corruption." This verse does not talk about David because he was buried with his fathers and saw corruption. Jesus was raised from the dead and saw no corruption; He fulfilled this Old Testament prophecy.

4. Paul's bold statement to the Jews is, "The word of God needed to be preached to you first, but since you reject it and consider yourselves unworthy of everlasting life, from now on, we will go to the Gentiles." The Jews exhibited jealousy because they were filled with envy by the large multitudes that gathered to listen. They exhibited pride because they did not humble themselves to receive the gospel and believed they were superior to the Gentiles. They were hungry for control and power because they did not want their teachings changed.

Chapter 23:

1. Paul and Barnabas decided to leave Iconium because the Gentiles, Jews, and rulers of the city planned to stone them.

2. The people of Lystra were astonished by the healing of the lame man and heralded Paul and Barnabas as gods. Paul and Barnabas, distressed by the people's reactions, tore their clothes, the Jewish reaction to blaspheming. They began to preach about the uselessness of idolatry and urged them to turn to the true God.

3. The Jews from Pisidian Antioch and Iconium stirred up the crowd, which caused their emotions toward Paul and Barnabas to change from reverence to hatred.

Chapter 24:

1. Paul knew seeking God's guidance was the most important step since they were doing His work. When God calls His people to a certain place or ministry, and they obey, He makes the work fruitful.

2. Paul advises Eutychus to have a willing heart so God can use him.

3. AWV. Paul and Barnabas argued that God's salvation was through grace for everyone, Jews and Gentiles alike, while the Jewish Christians argued that the Gentiles must be circumcised to be saved and must keep the law of Moses to be accepted.

Chapter 25:

1. AWV. Possible responses include asking God for humility, being ready to bear others' burdens, and sharing God's love. (An illustration of this mindset is two runners competing; when one falls, the other rushes to help him up, forfeiting the prize but looking out for the interests of his competitor. Pray and ask God to fill you with His humility and self-giving love

so you can look out for others!)

2. Peter had to understand that Jewish law could not be added to Jesus' offer of salvation by grace because if we are saved through the law, then Christ died in vain. We are not justified by the law but by grace alone!

3. John Mark learned that God's work was individual and personal, and his excitement should not come from large multitudes being saved but from God's work in individuals' hearts. He was inspired and convicted by the parable of the shepherd who left the ninety-nine for one and by the story of Jesus crossing the sea to save one sinner.

4. John Mark eventually wrote the gospel of Mark.

Chapter 26:

1. Timothy is described as a young man around the same age as Tychicus. His father is Greek, but his mother is Jewish. Timothy is also passionate about Scripture and expresses a desire to serve God. Timothy's family knew Paul from his first missionary journey, when he had visited Lystra and preached there before being stoned by the people. Timothy said that his words had been a blessing, and his boldness had inspired them. Paul was an instrument in helping Timothy's family understand the Scriptures better.

2. Paul responded that he was caught off guard initially, although he shouldn't have been surprised since the crowds hailed Jesus as their king just moments before they crucified Him.

3. Paul was not disappointed with God's change of direction. Rather, he felt blessed to be part of God's work. He was confident that God would always direct his steps and knew that perfect peace was in the center of His will.

Chapter 27:

1. The doctor who treated Eutychus is named Doctor Luke. He wrote the book of Luke.

2. Dr. Luke was astounded that Eutychus was healed so suddenly without any medicine. He did not understand who Jesus was and why Paul prayed to Him.

3. Paul knew that God was directing the group to Macedonia because he received a night vision in which a Macedonian man stood and pleaded with Paul to "come over to Macedonia and help." This was a clear direction from God.

4. AWV. Paul explained baptism as an outward expression of faith, representing being buried with Christ and cleansed. Paul also mentioned that it was a commandment given by Jesus that all Christians were to obey.

Chapter 28:

1. Paul disapproved of the young girl's shouting because a spirit of Pythona possessed her, and he knew that God did not need demonic approval of His work.

2. The girl's slave masters were upset that their only hope of profit was gone, so they told the magistrates that they were troubling the city and teaching Jewish customs that were not lawful for Romas to observe.

3. The disciples prayed the whole night for Paul and Silas. The miracles the Lord did were that Paul and Silas had joy in the prison, there was an earthquake that broke their chains, none of the prisoners fled, the jailer's heart was open to receive the gospel, the jailer was compassionate to tend to their wounds, the jailer's whole family was baptized, and the magistrates apologized and pled for them to leave the city.

4. The devil intended to harm Paul and Silas by having them beaten and throwing them in prison. God used that situation

for good to spread salvation to the jailer's family.

5. The magistrates had beaten Paul and Silas openly when they were uncondemned Romans, an act punishable by death. The magistrates couldn't simply send them away without acknowledging their error.

6. Paul wrote the book of Philippians for the church in Philippi.

Chapter 29:

1. Since the Bereans were genuine listeners, Paul wanted to leave them with someone to help them grow.

2. With the inscription "TO THE UNKNOWN GOD" on one of the idols, Paul could speak about the God they didn't know, Jesus. The God they were unwittingly seeking is the Creator of heaven and earth and does not dwell in temples made with hands. He is the source of life for all nations!

3. Paul quoted the words of the major prophet, Ezekiel.

Chapter 30:

1. The Lord promised Paul that no one in Corinth would attack him to hurt him, for He had many people in that city. This gave Paul the boldness to speak the gospel to the people, called the Corinthians. The two epistles written to them are 1st and 2nd Corinthians.

2. Gallio refused to judge Paul because he had not committed a criminal offense. It was a matter of words, names, and the Jewish law, which Gallio did not want to judge.

3. Nothing can stop God's work! AWV. Encourage a positive response.

Chapter 31:

1. Paul followed the Nazarite vow, in which a person grows their hair for some time before cutting it off and offering it to the Lord at a special ceremony. Paul used this traditional Jewish way to express his gratitude toward God.

2. Eutychus had called the disciples' house in Jerusalem, the church gatherings in Antioch, and the houses they lodged at in foreign countries his home. However, going back to his home in Beth-Zayit felt different to him.

3. Silvanus left home to find a job, which frustrated his father because he expected Silvanus to stay and care for him in his old age. Silvanus was supposed to inherit the family farm, but he had left to search for a greater purpose in life. Silvanus' father felt burdened by Silvanus seemingly abandoning them for something more rewarding.

4. Eutychus decided to keep the whistle Silvanus had carved for him, hoping he would see his best friend again.

Chapter 32:

1. Paul explained that John's baptism was already fulfilled through Jesus. The disciples at Ephesus understood who Jesus was and received the Holy Spirit.

2. When Paul could no longer teach in the synagogue, he gathered the disciples together privately in the school of Tyrannus.

3. Many people took Paul's handkerchiefs and aprons and laid them on the sick, and they were healed. The sons of Sceva tried to imitate Paul, but they did not have a relationship with Jesus, so it backfired on them. Many local magicians were astonished and convicted by Paul's preaching, so they confessed their deeds and burned their magic books.

4. Paul wrote the book of Ephesians to the church at Ephesus.

Chapter 33:

1. Demetrius was offended when Paul said that the gods made with hands are not real. What was ironic about his anger was that he was the one making the images, so he should have known they were not real. His viewpoint was very sad because he got angry when Paul stated the obvious and feared the loss of business rather than fearing God and eternal condemnation.

2. AWV. Some examples of chaotic behavior include a cacophony of words and languages that Eutychus described on page 241. The Ephesians also seized Paul's travel companions and brought them into the amphitheater, where the protests were unintelligible because of the echoes. Most of the Ephesians did not know why they were gathered. This riot continued for two hours.

3. The city clerk told them that they needed to be quiet since it could not be denied that Ephesus was the guardian of their goddess, Diana. They had caused a commotion because of men who did not rob their temple or blaspheme their goddess. If Demetrius had a problem with Paul, the city clerk said he could bring him to court to determine everything in an organized assembly. They had no reason to give for a disorderly gathering, and if Rome heard of the uproar, they would be punished.

Chapter 34:

1. Paul returned through Macedonia instead because the Jews were trying to kill him.

2. Uncle Elijah wore long, flowing robes dyed richly. His house was described as stately, with ornate, intricately designed pillars and marble walkways. He also had gardens with numerous fruit trees and a fountain in the courtyard. He had

large stables with dozens of stalls and multiple horses. He had rugs with golden embroidery and a large library with a vast collection of scrolls.

3. Eutychus' father developed a deeper relationship with Jesus Christ, his Savior, and understood He was the promised Messiah. It wasn't about religion or following rituals to Him, but it was about knowing God. The laws helped him understand his sinfulness; they also helped him believe that Jesus was the Messiah because of all the prophecies He fulfilled. Eutychus' father summarized his view on the law by saying, "God has given us the law, but through faith in Him, we do not need to be governed by it."

Chapter 35:
1. AWV.

2. Eutychus said he wouldn't have changed any of his difficult travel experiences because, through those situations, God had taught him valuable lessons, such as His leading in Eutychus' life and His power over sin.

3. Eutychus' father said that not everyone who came to their church was a Christian; only those who committed to follow the Lord and had a personal relationship with God were His followers. Uncle Elijah had not confessed that Jesus was the only Lord over his life.

Chapter 36:
1. Paul was motivated by the privilege to participate in God's work. We should share the gospel because we can't keep quiet about God's goodness and want to share His truth with others.

2. Page 262.

3. AWV. Eutychus fell out of a window and received a second chance at life. Through this event, he found his window of opportunity and became a window for God's life to shine through.

Chapter 37:

1. Doctor Luke said Eutychus was "ignari" and "mortuus," which means unconscious and dead.

2. Eutychus realized that his life was truly in God's hands, and he had nothing to fear because God decided his future. God had given him a second chance at life and individually revealed His purpose to Eutychus. Knowing that he was alive for a reason gave him courage and confidence.

3. Eutychus advised Silvanus to read the Scriptures after becoming a Christian to understand God better. He also advised him to pray and develop a relationship with God.

4. Eutychus' favorite saying of Paul's is that God uses a willing heart.

5. AWV. The author prays that you will continue to study His word and will be inspired to be a bold witness for Him. May you have a willing heart to be used by God!

Made in the USA
Las Vegas, NV
14 November 2024

11789468R00030